WORLD OF INSECTS

Ladybugs

by Martha E. H. Rustad

BELLWETHER MEDIA • MINNEAPOLIS, MN

BLASTOFF!
2
READERS

Note to Librarians, Teachers, and Parents:

Blastoff! Readers are carefully developed by literacy experts and combine standards-based content with developmentally-appropriate text.

Level 1 provides the most support through repetition of high-frequency words, light text, predictable sentence patterns, and strong visual support.

Level 2 offers early readers a bit more challenge through varied simple sentences, increased text load, and less repetition of high frequency words.

Level 3 advances early-fluent readers toward fluency through increased text and concept load, less reliance on visuals, longer sentences, and more literary language.

Level 4 builds reading stamina by providing more text per page, increased use of punctuation, greater variation in sentence patterns, and increasingly challenging vocabulary.

Level 5 encourages children to move from "learning to read" to "reading to learn" by providing even more text, varied writing styles, and less familiar topics.

Whichever book is right for your reader, Blastoff! Readers are the perfect books to build confidence and encourage a love of reading that will last a lifetime!

This edition first published in 2008 by Bellwether Media.

Library of Congress Cataloging-in-Publication Data
Rustad, Martha E. H. (Martha Elizabeth Hillman), 1975–
   Ladybugs / by Martha E. H. Rustad.
      p. cm. – (Blastoff! readers : world of insects)
   Summary: "Simple text accompanied by full-color photographs give an upclose look at ladybugs. Intended for kindergarten through third grade students"—Provided by publisher.
   Includes bibliographical references and index.
   ISBN-13: 978-1-60014-077-8 (hardcover : alk. paper)
   ISBN-10: 1-60014-077-7 (hardcover : alk. paper)
   1. Ladybugs—Juvenile literature. I. Title.
   QL596.C65R87 2008
   595.76'9—dc22
                                        2007007468

Contents

Ladybugs are **insects**.
They are a kind of **beetle**.

Ladybugs hatch from eggs in spring.

Baby ladybugs are called **larva**. A ladybug larva is long and **spiny**.

Its favorite food is **aphids**.
Aphids are **pests** that
kill plants.

A larva eats and grows for 3 or 4 weeks. Then it builds a shell around its body.

Its body changes inside the shell. Soon an adult ladybug hatches.

Most adult ladybugs start out yellow. They do not have spots.

Soon their bodies may change color. Many turn red or orange with spots.

jaws

Ladybugs have strong **jaws** for chewing.

They can eat up to 50 insects
per day.

antennas

Ladybugs use **antennas** to feel and smell.

Their antennas help them find aphids.

All insects have six legs.
Ladybugs have a **claw**
on each leg.

Ladybugs grab aphids with their claws.

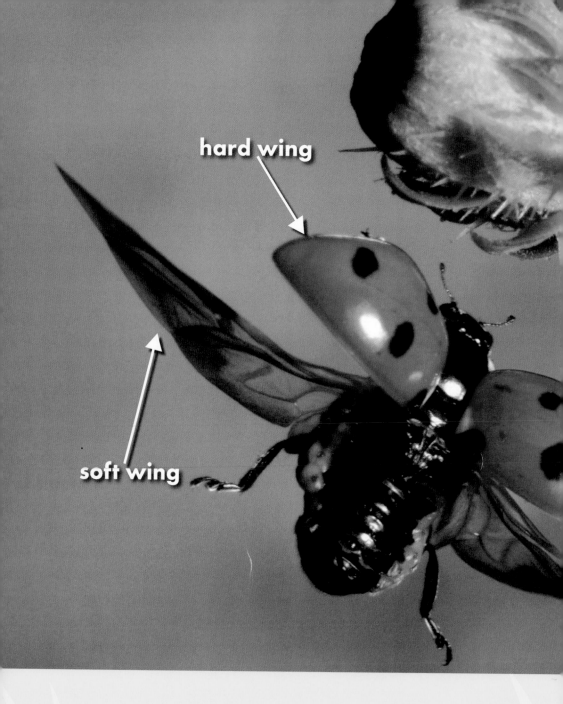

hard wing

soft wing

Ladybugs have two hard
wings and two soft wings.
They fly with their soft wings.

18

The hard wings cover and protect the soft wings.

Ladybugs gather together in fall. They find a safe place to rest for winter.

Ladybugs lay eggs in spring. Soon new ladybugs will hatch from the eggs.

Glossary

antennas—a pair of thin feelers on an insect's head; ladybugs use their antennas to find food.

aphid—a tiny insect that sucks juices from plants; aphids harm many food crops.

beetle—an insect with two hard wings and two soft wings; the world has more beetles than any other kind of animal.

claw—a sharp hook on the leg of an insect

insect—a kind of animal with six legs; most insects also have a hard body, two antennas, and two or four wings.

jaw—a sharp part on the mouth of an insect; ladybugs have jaws that move from side to side.

larva—a worm-like insect; a larva is the first stage of life for many insects; a ladybug larva is also called a grub.

pests—animals or plants that damage crops

spiny—covered with sharp points

To Learn More

AT THE LIBRARY

Allen, Judy. *Are You a Ladybug?* Backyard Books. New York: Kingfisher, 2000.

Llewellyn, Claire. *Ladybug*. Chanhassen, Minn.: NorthWord Press, 2004.

Loewen, Nancy. *Spotted Beetles: Ladybugs in Your Backyard*. Minneapolis, Minn.: Picture Window Books, 2004.

ON THE WEB

Learning more about ladybugs is as easy as 1, 2, 3.

1. Go to www.factsurfer.com

2. Enter "ladybugs" into search box.

3. Click the "Surf" button and you will see a list of related web sites.

With factsurfer.com, finding more information is just a click away.

Index

The photographs in this book are reproduced through the courtesy of: arlindo71, front cover, p. 14; Andrew Palmer/Alamy, pp. 4-5; blickwinkel/Alamy, pp. 6-7, 9; Hans Pfletschinger/Getty Images, p. 8; Christine van Reeuwyk, p. 10; Cre8tive Images, p. 11; pixelman, p. 12; George Grall/Getty Images, p. 13; Emilia Stasiak, p. 15; Martin Ruegner/Getty Images, p. 16; Keith Naylor, p.17; imagebroker/Alamy, pp. 18-19; Steve Shoup, p. 20; Nic Hamilton, p. 21.